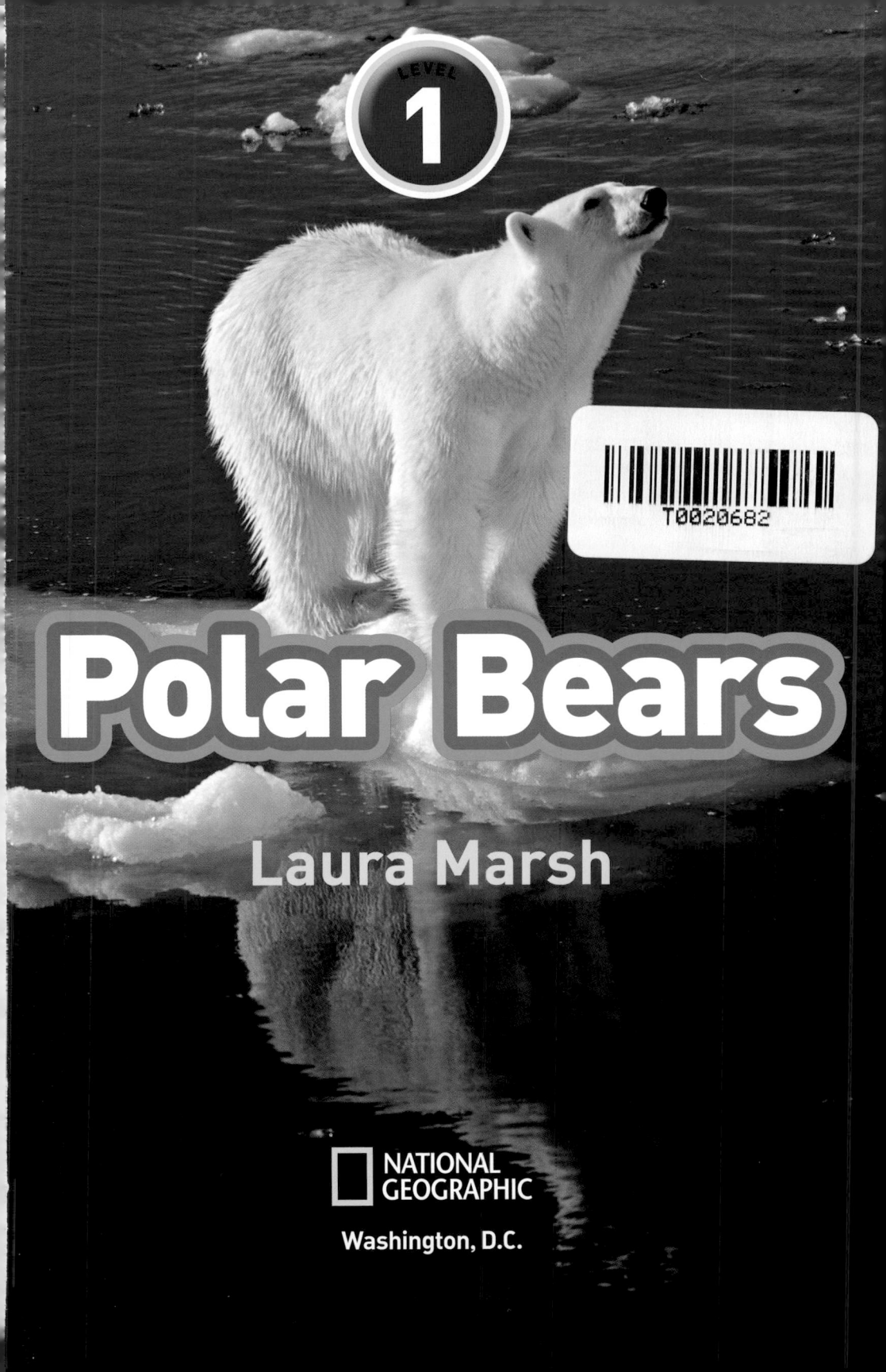
LEVEL
1
T0020682
Polar Bears
Laura Marsh
NATIONAL
GEOGRAPHIC
Washington, D.C.

For Eva —L. F. M.

The publisher and author gratefully acknowledge the expert assistance of Geoff York of WWF Canada.

Published by National Geographic Partners, LLC, Washington, DC 20036.

Copyright © 2013 National Geographic Society. All rights reserved. Reproduction of the whole or any part of the contents without written permission from the publisher is prohibited.

NATIONAL GEOGRAPHIC and Yellow Border Design are trademarks of the National Geographic Society, used under license.

Book design by YAY! Design

Paperback ISBN: 978-1-4263-1104-8
Library ISBN: 978-1-4263-1105-5

Photo Credits
Cover, Klein-Hubert/Kimball Stock; 1, Judith Conning/National Geographic Your Shot; 2, Steven Kazlowski/Nature Picture Library; 4, Ralph Lee Hopkins/National Geographic Image Collection; 6, Hemis/Alamy; 7, Siddhardha Gargie/National Geographic Your Shot; 8, Steven Kazlowski/Nature Picture Library; 9, Steven Kazlowski/Nature Picture Library; 10, Michael Weber/SuperStock; 12, ZSSD/Minden Pictures; 14, SuperStock; 15, Flip Nicklin/Minden Pictures; 16, Alaska Stock/Alamy; 16-17, Richard Ress/National Geographic Your Shot; 18, Matthias Breiter/Minden Pictures; 20, Rolf Hicker Photography/Alamy; 22 (UP), gary718/Shutterstock; 22 (CTR), Matt Propert/National Geographic Partners; 22 (LO), Christopher Drake/National Geographic Your Shot; 23 (UP LE), EcoStock/Shutterstock; 23 (UP RT), Flip Nicklen/Minden Pictures; 23 (LO LE), primopiano/Shutterstock; 23 (LO RT), John Conrad/Getty Images; 24, Jenny E. Ross/Getty Images; 25, Matthias Breiter/Minden Pictures; 26, T.J. Rich/Nature Picture Library; 28 (UP), Daniel J Cox/Getty Images; 28 (LO), AFP/Getty Images; 29, Linda Drake/National Geographic Your Shot; 30 (LE), Keith Levit Photography RF/Getty Images/Jupiter Images; 30 (RT), Valerie Abbott/National Geographic Your Shot; 31 (UP LE), Sergey Rusakov/Shutterstock; 31 (UP RT), Matt Propert; 31 (LO LE), Pradeep Chitta/National Geographic Your Shot; 31 (LO RT), Vladimir Melnik/Shutterstock; 32 (UP LE), Fedorov Oleksiy/Shutterstock; 32 (UP RT), Flip Nicklin/National Geographic Stock; 32 (LO LE), Andy Barnes/National Geographic Your Shot; 32 (LO RT), Uryadnikov Sergey/Shutterstock; header used throughout, Nebojsa S/Shutterstock

Collection ISBN (Paperback): 978-1-4263-1522-0
Collection ISBN (Library Edition): 978-1-4263-1612-8

Printed in the United States of America
23/QCG/10

Table of Contents

Who Am I? 4
Big Bears! 6
Powerful Paws 10
Super Swimmers 12
What's for Dinner? 14
Bears in Town 20
7 Amazing Polar Bear Facts 22
Cute Cubs 24
Playtime! 28
What in the World? 30
Picture Glossary 32

Who Am I?

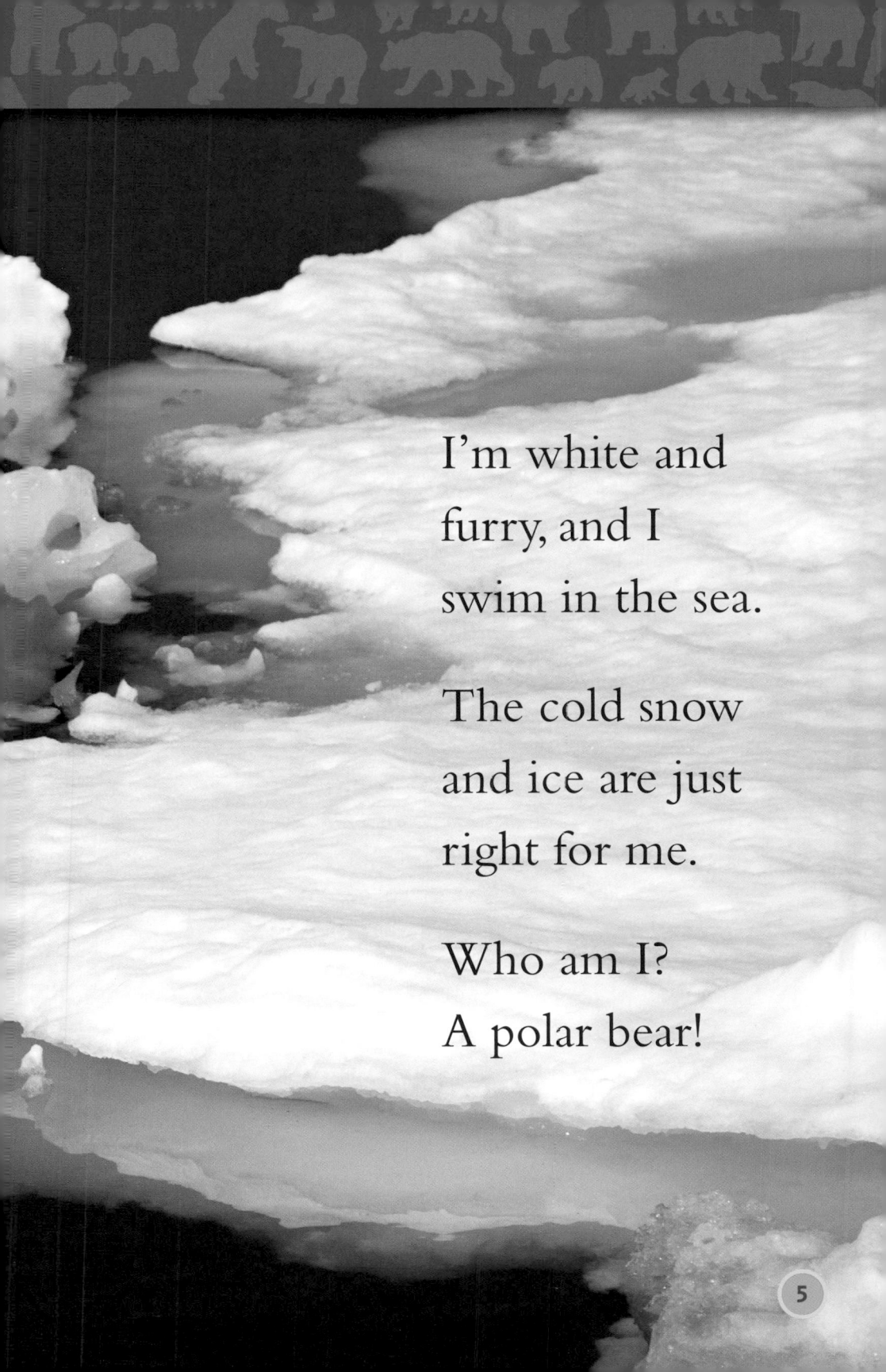

I'm white and
furry, and I
swim in the sea.

The cold snow
and ice are just
right for me.

Who am I?
A polar bear!

Big Bears!

Have you seen a polar bear in a zoo? Polar bears are big—really big.

They are the biggest meat-eaters on land. A polar bear can weigh as much as seven men!

A polar bear's body is built for the Arctic. These bears have thick fur to keep them warm.

Polar bears have thick fat, too. The fat keeps body heat in and keeps the Arctic cold out.

Q How do polar bears stay cool?

A They turn on bear conditioning!

Word Bite

ARCTIC: The area near the North Pole, where it is very cold

Powerful Paws
Long, thick, curved claws grab food easily.
Thick pads keep feet warm.
Bumps on the footpads keep bears from slipping on the ice.
Front paws are webbed, like ducks' feet. This helps polar bears swim.

Big paws keep bears from sinking into the snow. The paws are larger than a dinner plate!

A polar bear's paws do many things. Paws dig dens in the snow. They break the ice to find food. They also pull food out of the water.

Word Bite

DEN: A hidden hole where a wild animal lives. Polar bear mothers have their babies in a den.

Super Swimmers

Polar bears are great swimmers. They spend a lot of time in the water.

Their front paws paddle. Their back legs steer. Their fat helps polar bears float.

Word Bite

FLOAT: To rest or move in water without sinking

What's for Dinner?

A polar bear eats other animals. Seals are its favorite food. This bear is hunting seals on the sea ice.

Q What do polar bears eat for lunch?

A Ice berg-ers!

Seals come up for air at holes in the ice. The bear waits and waits. Finally, a seal appears. The polar bear snatches it in a flash.

Polar bears have good noses. They can smell a seal 20 miles away!

Polar bears have good hearing and eyesight, too. These come in handy when looking for dinner. This bear has spotted an arctic fox.

The ice melts in spring and summer. Polar bears stay with the ice when they can. They move to land when the sea ice is mostly gone.

On land they usually don't eat at all. Some bears may eat bird eggs. They may eat plants or berries. But there is not much food for polar bears on land.

Q Where do polar bears keep their money?

A In snow banks.

Bears in Town

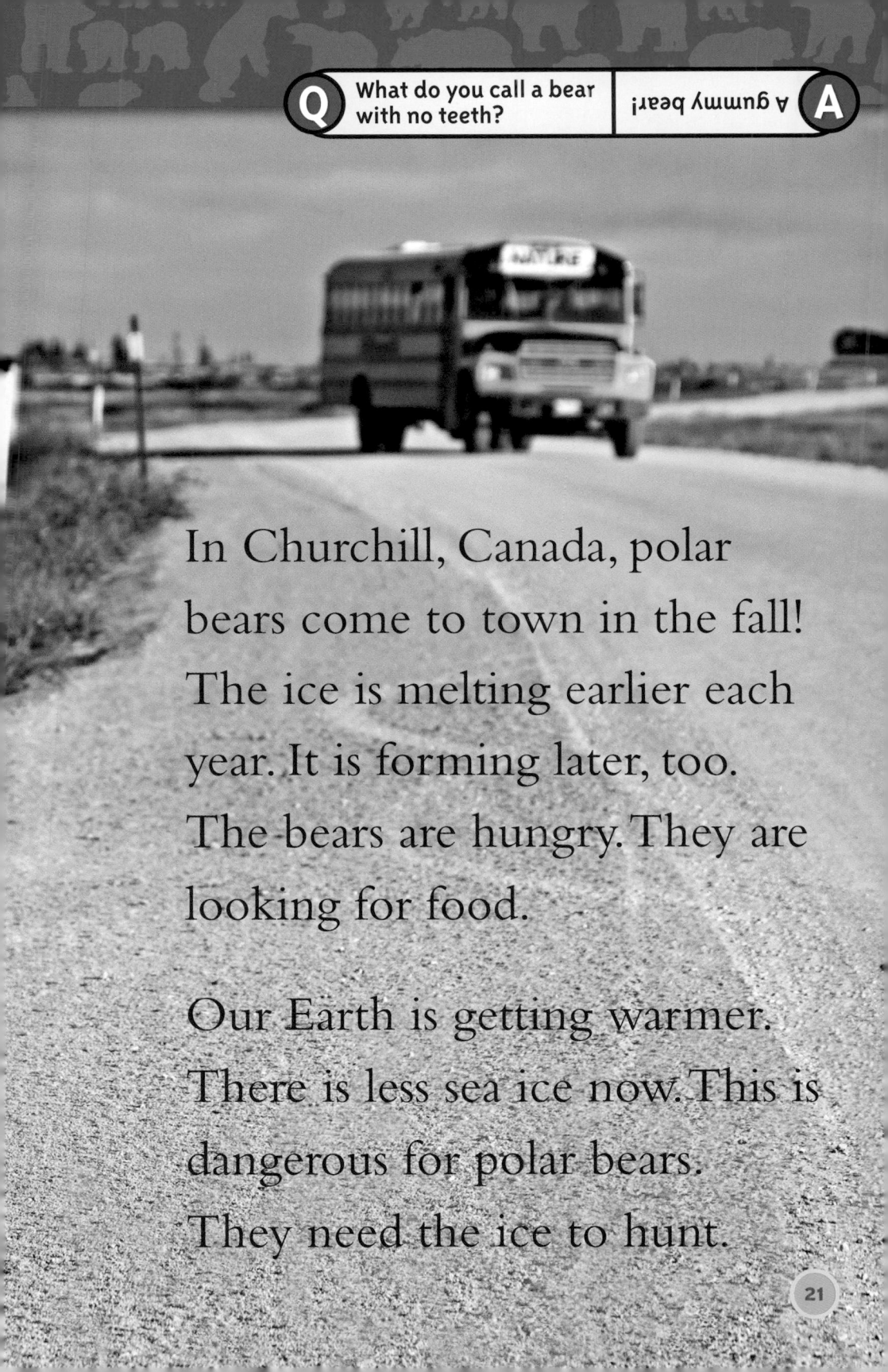

Q What do you call a bear with no teeth?

A A gummy bear!

In Churchill, Canada, polar bears come to town in the fall! The ice is melting earlier each year. It is forming later, too. The bears are hungry. They are looking for food.

Our Earth is getting warmer. There is less sea ice now. This is dangerous for polar bears. They need the ice to hunt.

7 Amazing Polar Bear Facts

1

The largest polar bear ever recorded was 2,209 pounds. That's the weight of a small sports car!

2

Polar bears have black skin underneath their white fur.

3

Sometimes polar bears get too hot. Then they take a swim or roll in the snow.

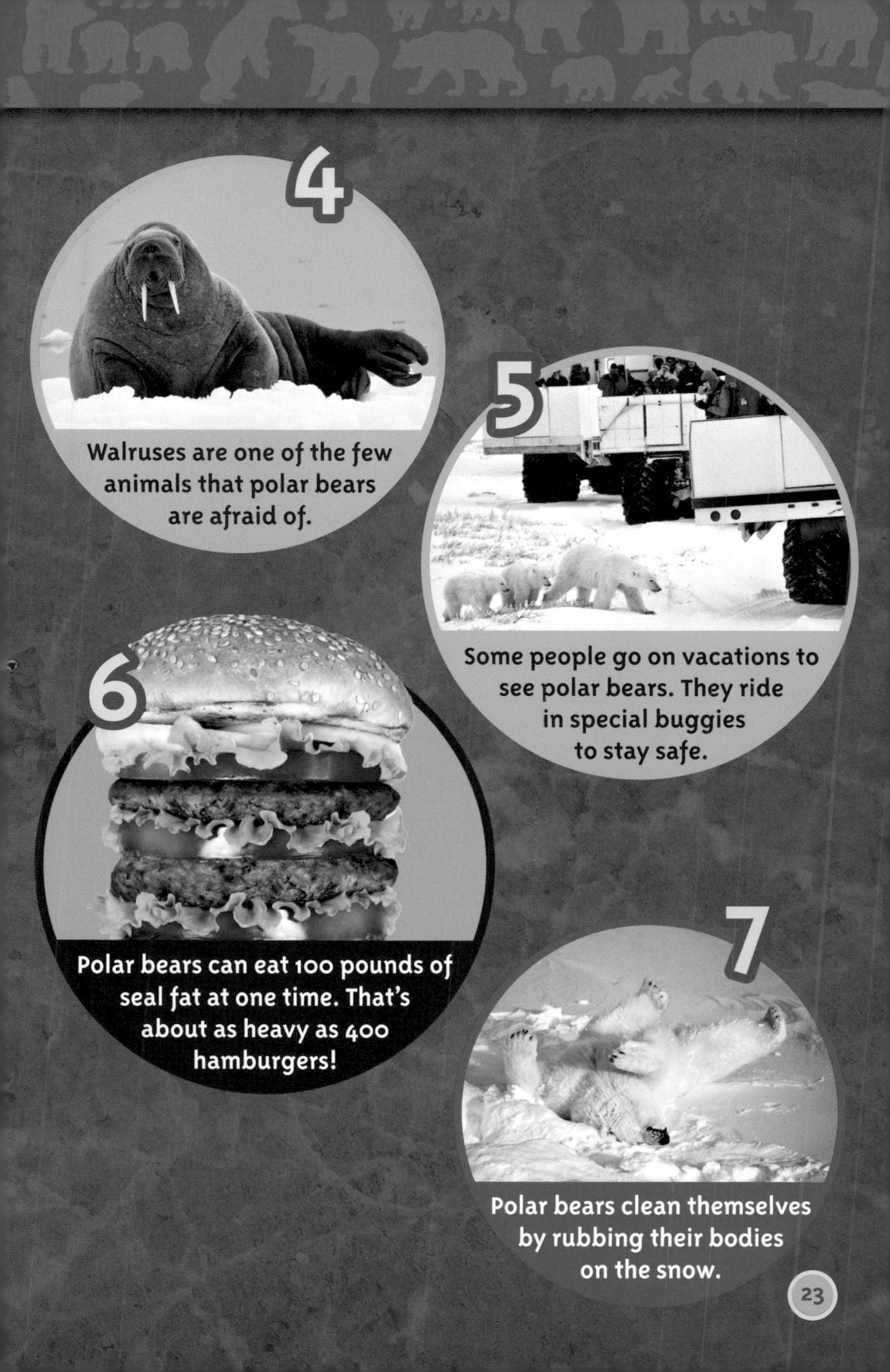

4

Walruses are one of the few animals that polar bears are afraid of.

5

Some people go on vacations to see polar bears. They ride in special buggies to stay safe.

6

Polar bears can eat 100 pounds of seal fat at one time. That's about as heavy as 400 hamburgers!

7

Polar bears clean themselves by rubbing their bodies on the snow.

Cute Cubs

Every new polar bear is special. A mother bear has babies, called cubs. She digs a den in the snow. The cubs stay safe and warm in the den.

The cubs drink their mother's rich milk. They grow quickly. Soon they are big enough to leave the den.

A mother polar bear teaches her cubs to hunt. She also teaches them how to stay safe and warm.

Q Why do polar bears have fur coats?

A Because they look silly in jackets!

The cubs leave their mother when they are two years old. They are ready to live on their own.

Playtime!

Polar bears like to play just like you!

Bears wrestle with each other. They slide in the snow. They like to play games, too.

Q What is a polar bear's favorite breakfast?

A Ice Crispies!

Sometimes a cub gets a ride from Mom! These bears are off on an Arctic adventure.

What in the World?

These pictures show up-close views of things in a polar bear's world. Use the hints to figure out what's in the pictures. Answers are on page 31.

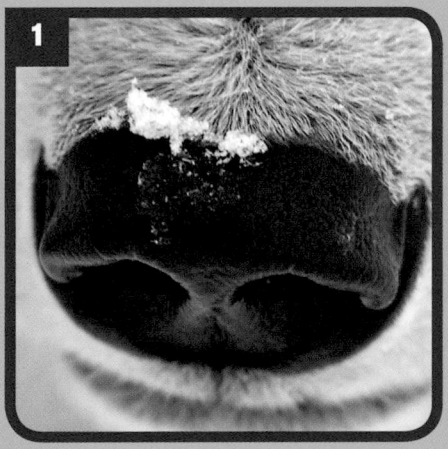

HINT: Helps find dinner

HINT: You don't have one of these.

WORD BANK

Walrus Paw Tail Nose Fur Seal

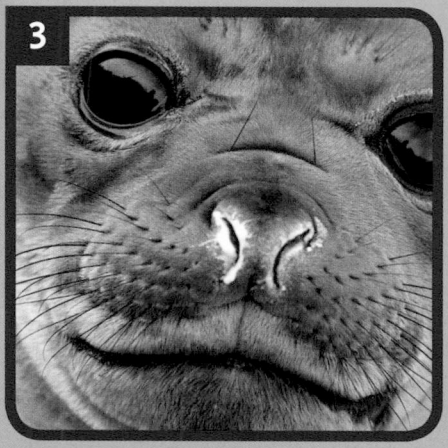

HINT: A polar bear's favorite food

HINT: Keeps a bear warm

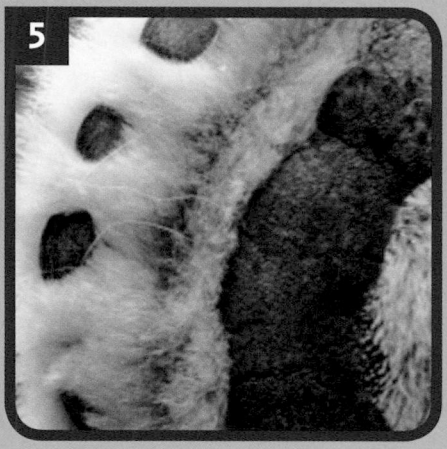

HINT: Built for snow, ice, and water

HINT: Polar bears are afraid of this animal.

Answers: 1. Nose, 2. Tail, 3. Seal, 4. Fur, 5. Paw, 6. Walrus

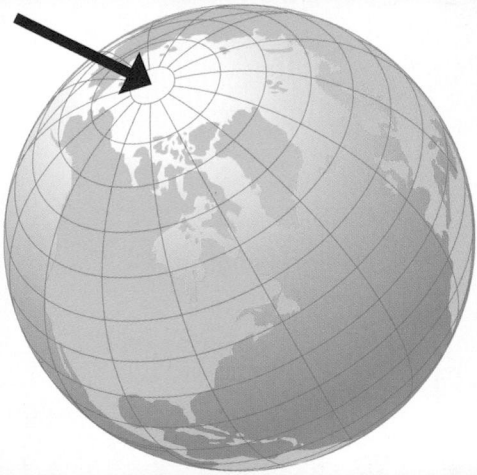

ARCTIC: The area near the North Pole, where it is very cold

CUB: A baby bear

DEN: A hidden hole where a wild animal lives. Polar bear mothers have their babies in a den.

FLOAT: To rest or move in water without sinking

LEVEL
2
Monkeys
Anne Schreiber
NATIONAL
GEOGRAPHIC
Washington, D.C.

To Jacob, Sammy, and Noah—a barrel of monkeys!
—A. S.

The publisher and author gratefully acknowledge the review of proofs for this book by Joe Knobbe of the Saint Louis Zoo and Keith Lovett of the Palm Beach Zoo.

Published by National Geographic Partners, LLC, Washington, DC 20036.

Copyright © 2013 National Geographic Society

All rights reserved. Reproduction of the whole or any part of the contents without written permission from the publisher is prohibited.

NATIONAL GEOGRAPHIC and Yellow Border Design are trademarks of the National Geographic Society, used under license.

ISBN: 978-1-4263-1106-2 (Trade paper)
ISBN: 978-1-4263-1107-9 (Library)

Design by YAY! Design

Photo Credits
Cover, Elio Della Ferrera/Nature Picture Library; 1, Josh Brown/National Geographic Your Shot/National Geographic Image Collection; 2, Imagewerks Japan/Getty Images; 4-5, Brad Starry/National Geographic Your Shot/National Geographic Image Collection; 7 (UP LE), Pete Oxford/Minden Pictures; 7 (UP RT), Fiona Rogers/Nature Picture Library; 7 (LO), Chiangkunta/Flickr RM/Getty Images; 8, Thomas Marent/ Minden Pictures/Getty Images; 9, Danita Delimont/Alamy; 10-11, Marsel van Oosten/Squiver; 13 (UP LE), Thomas Marent/Visuals Unlimited, Inc./Getty Images; 13 (UP RT), Judith Arsenault/National Geographic Your Shot/National Geographic Image Collection; 13 (LE CTR), Anup Shah; 13 (RT CTR), Jennifer Kraft/National Geographic Your Shot/National Geographic Image Collection; 13 (LO LE), Dr. Clive Bromhall/Getty Images; 13 (LO RT), Judith Arsenault/National Geographic Your Shot/National Geographic Image Collection; 14, Jerry Young/Dorling Kindersley; 15, Eric Isselée/Shutterstock; 16, Christianne Lagura/National Geographic Image Collection; 17, Thomas Marent/Minden Pictures/Getty Images; 18, Donna Tramontozzi/National Geographic Your Shot/National Geographic Image Collection; 19, Bruno D'Amicis/Nature Picture Library; 20, Pete Oxford/Minden Pictures/Getty Images; 22, SA Team/Foto Natura/Minden Pictures; 23, Pornchai Kittiwongsakul/AFP/Getty Images; 24 (UP), Mario Tizon/National Geographic Your Shot/National Geographic Image Collection; 24 (CTR), Cathleen Burnham/National Geographic Your Shot/National Geographic Image Collection; 24 (LO), AP Photo/Public Library of Science, Maurice Emetshu; 25 (UP), Anup Shah/Getty Images; 25 (CTR), Frank Lukasseck/Getty Images; 25 (LO), Mint Images-Frans Lanting/Getty Images; 26-27, Cyril Ruoso/JH Editorial/Minden Pictures/Getty Images; 28, Mattias Klum/National Geographic Image Collection; 29, Barbara Walton/epa/Shutterstock; 30 (UP), Karl Ammann/Digital Vision; 30 (CTR), Matt Propert/National Geographic Partners; 30 (LO), Jeremy Phan/National Geographic Your Shot/ National Geographic Image Collection; 31 (UP LE), James Pelton/National Geographic Your Shot/National Geographic Image Collection; 31 (UP RT), Branislav Bieleny/National Geographic Your Shot/National Geographic Image Collection; 31 (LE CTR), M Rutherford/Shutterstock; 31 (RT CTR), Sebastien Barreau/National Geographic Your Shot/National Geographic Image Collection; 31 (LO LE), Andrey Pavlov/Shutterstock; 31 (LO RT), HakueiHuang/National Geographic Your Shot/National Geographic Image Collection; 32 (UP LE), Anna Kucherova/Shutterstock; 32 (UP RT), Jeff Mauritzen/National Geographic Partners; 32 (LE CTR), Cyril Ruoso/JH Editorial/Minden Pictures/Getty Images; 32 (RT CTR), Galyna Andrushko/Shutterstock; 32 (LO LE), worldswildlifewonders/Shutterstock; 32 (LO RT), Dr. CliveBromhall/Getty Images; art in running head, stock09/Shutterstock; art in "Monkey Talk" boxes, Brad Collett/Shutterstock

Table of Contents

Monkey Business. 4

Monkeying Around. 6

All in the Family. 12

Monkey Babies. 16

Tools of the Trade 20

Want a Banana?. 22

6 Marvelous Monkeys. 24

Friends and Family. 26

Monkeys in Trouble. 28

Stump Your Parents 30

Glossary 32

Monkey Business

Yellow baboons

Who spends their
days climbing in trees,
leaping up high or
swinging with ease?

Who calls out in
grunts, screeches,
or whoops?

Who lives together in
groups we call troops?

Monkeys, that's who!

Monkeying Around

Monkeys live in many different kinds of habitats. They live in jungles and on mountains. They live in rain forests, grasslands, and even in cities and towns.

Many monkeys are arboreal (ar-BOR-ee-ul) monkeys. That means they live in the trees. Other monkeys live mostly on the ground.

Monkey Talk

HABITAT: The place where a plant or animal lives in nature

Common marmoset
Gelada baboon
Macaque

Monkey Talk

CANOPY: The area high up in the trees

PREHENSILE: Made for grabbing hold, like some monkeys' tails

The spider monkey uses its strong, prehensile (pree-HEN-sil) tail to grab and hold on.

Q Why did the monkey go to jail?

A He got into a life of climb.

Life in the Trees

Many arboreal monkeys live in the canopy (KAN-uh-pee) layer of the trees. They move from branch to branch.

Why don't they fall? Some monkeys use their tails like a third arm. Other monkeys have pads on their bottoms to keep them in place.

A colobus monkey using its bottom pads to stay put

Ah, the Spa!

Snow monkeys are macaques (muh-KAKS). Many of them live in the mountains of Japan. These monkeys know how to warm up in the winter.

They bathe in the hot mountain water. The water is heated inside the Earth and bubbles to the surface. Snow monkeys like to relax and play in the warm water.

All in the Family

Monkeys and apes are both primates (PRY-mates). Primates are animals known for their big brains. They are smart. Their eyes face straight ahead. Sound like someone you know?

Surprise! Humans are primates, too. Humans are in the ape family! Chimpanzees, bonobos, orangutans, gibbons, gorillas, and humans are all apes.

Monkey Talk

PRIMATE: An animal with forward-facing eyes, grasping hands or tail, and handlike feet

Apes		Monkeys
 do not have tails	TAIL	 have tails
 usually larger, can walk on two legs	BODY	 usually smaller, walk on four legs
 very smart, most use tools	BRAIN	 smart, most do not use tools

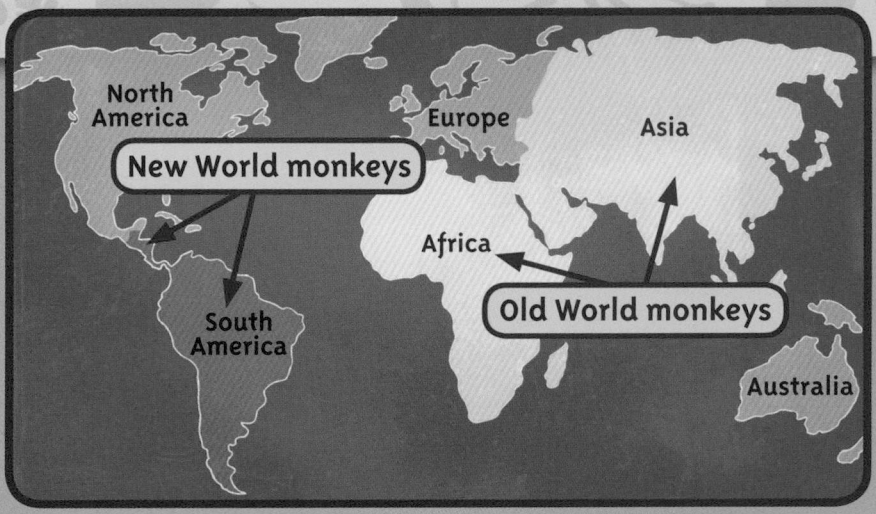

New World monkeys live in parts of Central and South America. They are small and have flat noses. They live in trees.

Capuchin monkeys live in parts of Central and South America.

Q What does a monkey like to eat on the run?

A A banana split.

Old World monkeys live in parts of Africa and Asia. They are larger, and their noses are not flat. They live in mountains, grasslands, forests, and towns. They sit on their bottom pads.

Vervet monkeys live in parts of Africa.

Monkey Babies

Monkey mothers have a strong bond with their babies. This bond helps babies learn from their mothers. Monkey babies stay close to their moms for the first year.

Monkey Talk

BOND:
A strong feeling between animals that makes them close. Mother and baby monkeys have a strong bond.

Young macaque

Silvered leaf monkeys

A newborn monkey holds on tight to its mother's front. Later, it rides on its mom's back.

Barbary macaques

Young monkeys play together. They wrestle and tumble. When boys are older, they usually go off to join another troop. Most girl monkeys stay with their moms. One day they will raise their own families.

Tools of the Trade

Brown capuchin

Q What do you get when you cross a jungle with an office?

A Monkey business.

Most monkeys don't use tools. But capuchin (KA-pyu-shen) monkeys do! They sometimes use tools to find food. They use rocks to dig up potatoes. They also use rocks to crack open nuts and seeds.

Rocks aren't the only tools these monkeys use. When capuchin monkeys need to protect themselves against snakes, they may use a tree branch as a club.

Want a Banana?

Do you have to eat your fruits and vegetables? Monkeys do, too!

Monkeys eat more than 200 different types of food.

Most monkeys eat plants such as seeds, leaves, and fruit, including bananas! Monkeys sometimes eat insects, too.

This Midas tamarin is eating seed pods.

Every year people in the city of Lopburi, Thailand, throw a party for the macaque monkeys that live there. People put out more than 4,000 pounds of food for the monkeys!

6 Marvelous Monkeys

Loudest!

Howler monkeys can be heard up to three miles away.

Tiniest!

The pygmy marmoset is the world's smallest monkey. It's about the size of a banana.

Newest Found!

The lesula monkey was just discovered in the Democratic Republic of the Congo in Africa.

Biggest!

A male mandrill can be three feet long. It weighs about 77 to 100 pounds. That's as big as a large dog.

Furriest!

Golden snub-nosed monkeys have thick fur to keep them warm. They live in the cold mountains of China.

Fastest!

Patas can run up to 35 miles an hour. That's as fast as a racehorse.

Friends and Family

Monkeys have strong bonds with the other members of their troop.

Grooming is the main way monkeys show they care. Mothers groom babies. Females groom other females. And couples groom each other.

Monkey Talk

GROOM: To clean, brush, and care for

Q Why did the monkey make new friends?

A He wanted to branch out.

Monkeys in Trouble

What animal is the biggest danger to monkeys? Humans!

We have cut down forests where monkeys live. Without forests, monkeys have no place to go.

Forests that have been cut down in Malaysia

Proboscis (proh-BOS-is) monkeys live in the jungles of Borneo. Only a few thousand of them are left in the world. The mangrove forests they need for food are disappearing.

But some people are working to protect the land where monkeys live. This will help keep these amazing animals in our world.

Stump Your Parents

Can your parents answer these questions about monkeys? You might know more than they do!

Answers are at the bottom of page 31.

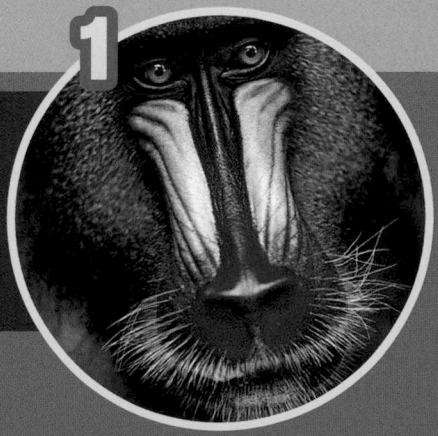

1

Where do monkeys live?

A. In cities
B. In forests
C. In jungles
D. All of the above

2

A monkey uses its prehensile tail to _____.

A. Fight
B. Sleep
C. Grab
D. Smell

3

Some monkeys are arboreal. Where do arboreal animals spend most of their time?

A. On the ground
B. In the air
C. In trees
D. Underwater

4

When a baby monkey is born, she _____.

A. Stays in her mother's pouch
B. Clings to her mother's front
C. Hangs from her mother's tail
D. Can immediately climb trees

5

Which animals are primates?

A. Monkeys
B. Great apes
C. Humans
D. All of the above

6

What do monkeys eat?

A. Bananas
B. Insects
C. Seeds
D. All of the above

7

What is the main way that monkeys show they care for each other?

A. They jump up and down.
B. They climb together.
C. They groom each other.
D. They play board games.

Answers: 1) D, 2) C, 3) C, 4) B, 5) D, 6) D, 7) C

BOND: A strong feeling between animals that makes them close. Mother and baby monkeys have a strong bond.

CANOPY: The area high up in the trees

GROOM: To clean, brush, and care for

HABITAT: The place where a plant or animal lives in nature

PREHENSILE: Made for grabbing hold, like some monkeys' tails

PRIMATE: An animal with forward-facing eyes, grasping hands or tail, and handlike feet

LEVEL
2
Penguins
Anne Schreiber
NATIONAL
GEOGRAPHIC
Washington, D.C.

To Hannah Sage and Hannah Rose
—A.S.

Published by National Geographic Partners, LLC, Washington, DC 20036.

Copyright © 2009 National Geographic Society

All rights reserved. Reproduction of the whole or any part of the contents without written permission from the publisher is prohibited.

NATIONAL GEOGRAPHIC and Yellow Border Design are trademarks of the National Geographic Society, used under license.

Library of Congress Cataloging-in-Publication Data
Schreiber, Anne.
Penguins! / Anne Schreiber.
p. cm.
ISBN 978-1-4263-0426-2 (pbk. : alk. paper) — ISBN 978-1-4263-0427-9 (library binding : alk. paper)
1. Penguins—Juvenile literature. I. Title.
QL696.S473S37 2009
598.47—dc22
2008022879

Photo Credits

Cover, Frans Lanting; 1, Marco Simoni/robertharding; 2, Bryan & Cherry Alexander/Viestiphoto; 4-5, Marc Chamberlain/Blue Planet Archive; 6-7, NG Maps; 8-9, Bill Curtsinger/National Geographic Image Collection; 8 (LE), Jerry Sharp/Shutterstock; 8 (RT), Fritz Polking/Gamma-Rapho via Getty Images; 9 (LE), Jurgita Genyte/Shutterstock; 9 (RT), WorldFoto/Alamy Stock Photo; 10-11, Paul Nicklen/National Geographic Image Collection; 12, Mike Lawrance/Alamy Stock Photo; 13, Martin Creasser/Alamy Stock Photo; 14-15, Seth Resnick/SuperStock; 14 (INSET), Paul Nicklen/National Geographic Image Collection; 16, Colin Monteath/Minden Pictures; 17, Kim Westerskov; 18, Maria Stenzel; 19, blickwinkel/Alamy Stock Photo; 20, Fuse/Getty Images; 21, Sue Flood; 22, Tim Davis; 23, Graham Robertson/Minden Pictures; 24-25, Paul Souders/Getty Images; 26-29 (BACKGROUND), Magenta/Alamy Stock Photo; 26 (UP LE), Susan Flashman/Shutterstock; 26 (UP CTR), Tui De Roy/Minden Pictures; 26 (UP RT), Barry Bland/Nature Picture Library; 26 (LO LE), Kevin Schafer/Alamy Stock Photo; 26 (LO RT), Tui De Roy/Minden Pictures; 27 (UP LE), W. Perry Conway/Getty Images; 27 (UP RT), Martin Pelanek/phototrip/Adobe Stock; 27 (LO LE), Sami Sarkis; 27 (LO RT), Zach Holmes/Alamy Stock Photo; 28 (UP LE), Konrad Wothe/Minden Pictures; 28 (UP RT), Tom Brakefield; 28 (LO LE), Ingrid Visser/Blue Planet Archive; 28 (LO RT), TJ Rich/Nature Picture Library; 29 (UP LE), W. Perry Conway/Getty Images; 29 (UP RT), Naturfoto-Online/Alamy Stock Photo; 29 (LO LE), Photodisc/Alamy Stock Photo; 29 (LO RT), Bryan & Cherry Alexander/Viestiphoto; 30, Solvin Zankl/Alamy Stock Photo; 31 (UP LE), Andy Rouse/Nature Picture Library; 31 (LO LE), Darrell Gulin/Getty Images; 31 (RT), David Tipling/Alamy Stock Photo; 32 (UP LE), Martin Creasser/Alamy Stock Photo; 32 (CTR LE), Colin Monteath/Minden Pictures; 32 (LO LE), Paul Nicklen/National Geographic Image Collection; 32 (CTR RT), NG Maps; 32 (LO RT), Jerry Sharp/Shutterstock

Table of Contents

What Are They? 4
Where Are They? 6
Not Just Any Bird 8
What's for Dinner? 12
Life on Land 16
A Chick Is Born 18
The Longest March 22
Penguin Parade 26
Penguin Play 30
Picture Glossary 32

What Are They?

EMPEROR PENGUINS

What birds cannot fly?
What birds spend most of their lives in the ocean but are not fish?
What birds live in the coldest part of the world — all year long?

They swim, they march, they slide through the snow.

They are penguins.

Where Are They?

BIRD WORDS

EQUATOR: An imaginary line halfway between the North and South Poles.

COAST: Where land meets water.

All penguins live between the Equator and the South Pole. Some live where it's very cold. Some live in warmer places like the coasts of Africa or Australia.

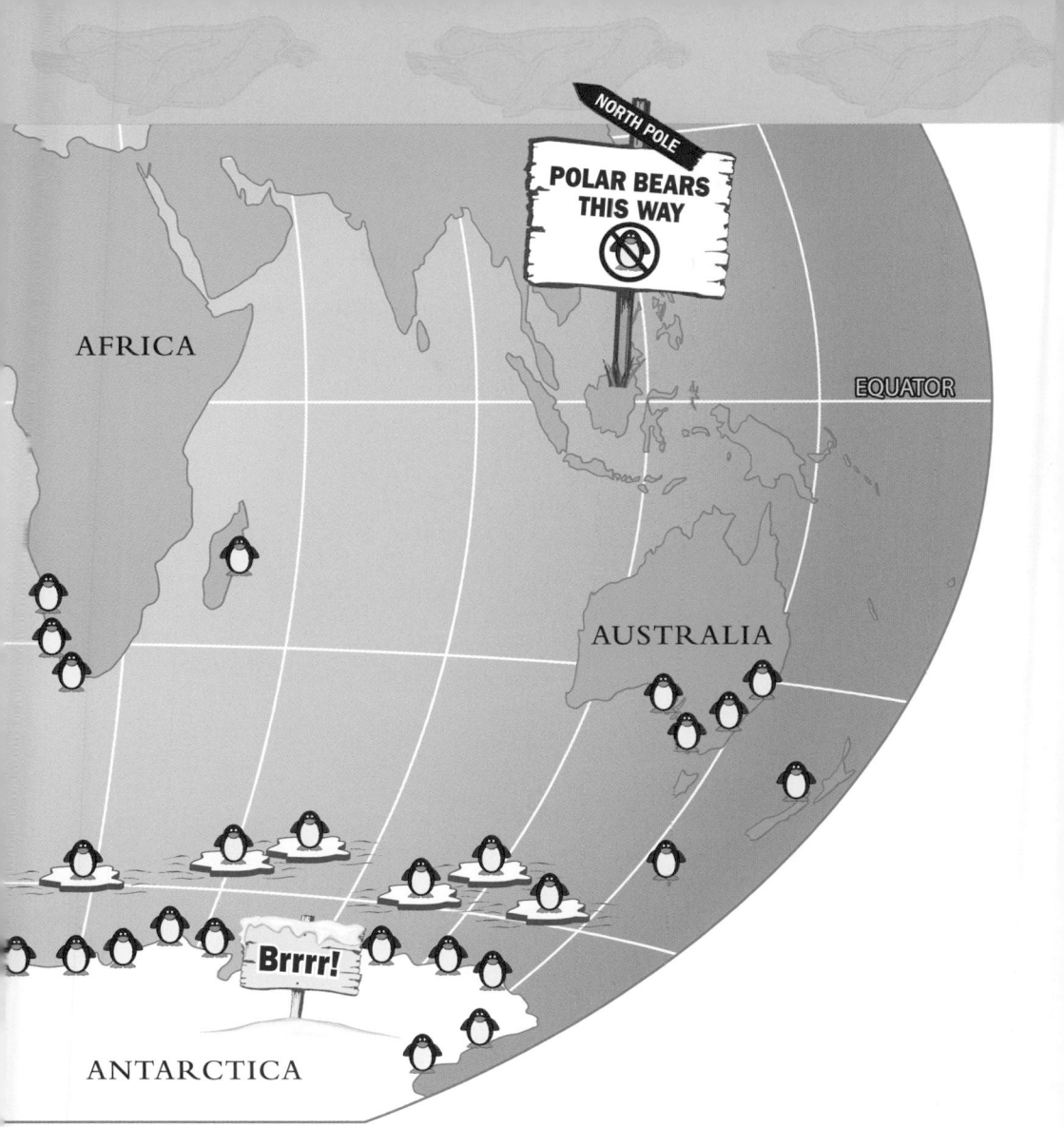

Penguins live on islands, on coasts, and even on icebergs in the sea. They just need to be near water, because they spend most of their lives IN the water.

Not Just Any Bird

Q What did the penguin do when he got upset?

A He *flippered* out.

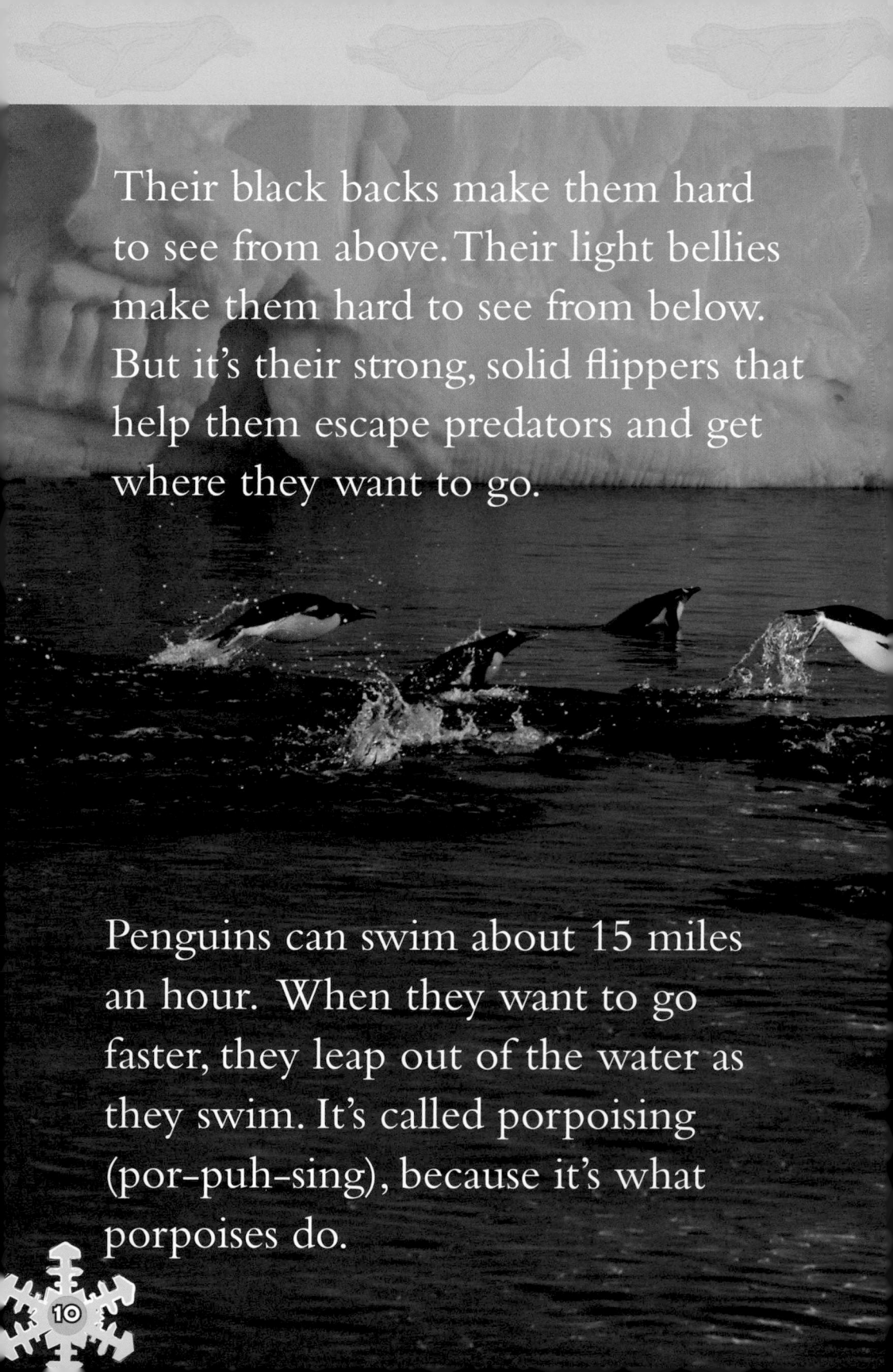

Their black backs make them hard to see from above. Their light bellies make them hard to see from below. But it's their strong, solid flippers that help them escape predators and get where they want to go.

Penguins can swim about 15 miles an hour. When they want to go faster, they leap out of the water as they swim. It's called porpoising (por-puh-sing), because it's what porpoises do.

Q Did the penguin leap out of the water by accident?

A No, he did it on *porpoise*.

A predator is an animal that eats other animals.

What's for Dinner?
HUMBOLDT PENGUIN

Q What's a penguin's favorite food?

A An *ice burger!*

Life in the ocean is fish-elicious! Penguins eat a lot of fish. They have a hooked bill, or beak, to help them grab their dinner. Barbs on their tongues and in their throats help them to hold on to slippery food.

Would you like a drink of salty water to go with that fish? Penguins are able to clean the salt out of ocean water. They get fresh water to drink and the salt dribbles back into the ocean.

BIRD WORDS

BARB: Something sharp and pointy like a hook.

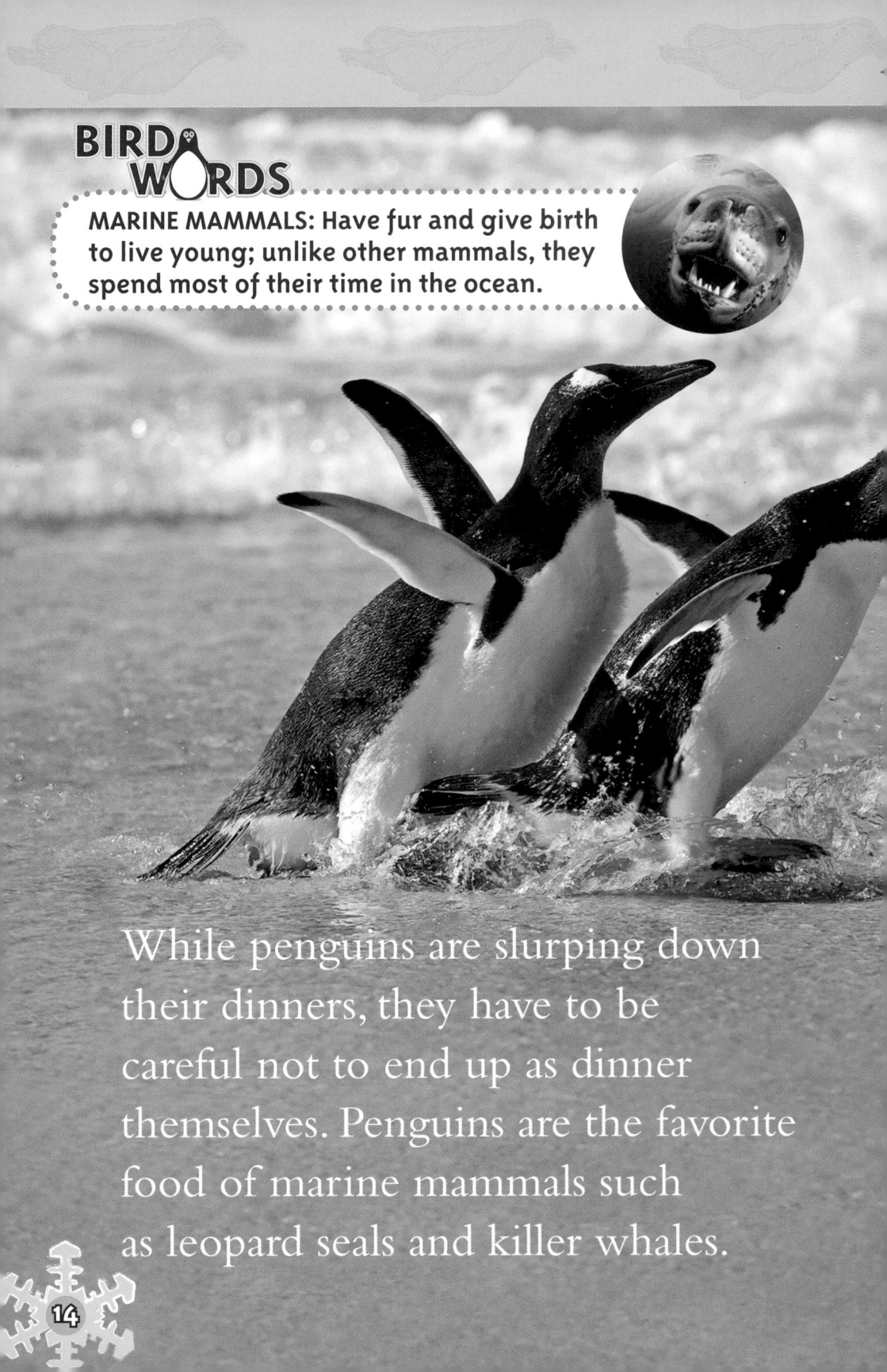

BIRD WORDS

MARINE MAMMALS: Have fur and give birth to live young; unlike other mammals, they spend most of their time in the ocean.

While penguins are slurping down their dinners, they have to be careful not to end up as dinner themselves. Penguins are the favorite food of marine mammals such as leopard seals and killer whales.

GENTOO PENGUINS AND A SKUA

Penguins are also in danger on land. Birds like the skua, the Australian sea eagle, and the giant petrel eat penguins. Even cats, snakes, foxes, and rats eat penguins when they can.

Life on Land

KING PENGUINS

BIRD WORDS

COLONY: A group of animals who live together.

On land, most penguins live in a large colony with thousands or even millions of other penguins. If it's cold, they huddle together. It's so warm inside a huddle that penguins take turns moving to the outside to cool off.

KING PENGUIN HUDDLE

Penguins march together to get to their nesting grounds. Once there they wave, strut, shake, call, nod, dance, and sing to find a mate. Most penguins stay with their mate for many years.

A Chick Is Born

CHINSTRAP CHICKS

Q How was the penguins' walk to their nesting grounds?

A *Egg*-cellent.

Most penguins lay two eggs at a time, but often only one egg survives. The mother and father take turns keeping the egg warm. When it hatches, the parents keep the chick warm and fed.

ADELIE CHICKS

After a couple of weeks, hundreds or even thousands of chicks wait together while the parents go back to the sea to find food. As the chicks wait, they are in constant danger from skuas, eagles, and other animals.

KING CHICK

Q What did the mother penguin say to her crying chick?

A "Stop *blubbering*."

GENTOO FEEDING CHICK

Finally, the parents return with food. They have to find their chicks in a huge crowd of baby birds. How do they do it? The baby birds sing special songs to help their parents find them.

In a few months, the whole family returns to the sea.

The Longest March

EMPEROR PENGUINS

For the emperor penguins, getting to their nesting grounds is hard work. Their home is Antarctica—the coldest place on Earth.

Emperor penguins nest much farther from the ocean than other penguins. They must march for days and nights through snow and wind.

After laying her egg, the female gives it to the male. He will keep it warm in a flap under his belly. Unlike other penguins, the male emperor cares for the egg by himself while the female goes back to the ocean to find food.

Q Who is the emperor penguin's favorite relative?

A *Aunt* Arctica.

The mother is gone for more than four months. The father huddles with the other male penguins to keep himself, and his egg, safe and warm. During this time, the father eats nothing but snow.

When the mother returns in July, the father quickly goes to the ocean to find food. By December, the whole family is ready to go.

Penguin Parade
Galapagos
HEIGHT
18″–21″
Fairy
HEIGHT
16″
SMALLEST
Fairy penguins sing more songs than any other penguins.
Snares
HEIGHT
21″–25″
Fiordland
HEIGHT
24″
Erect-Crested
HEIGHT
24″–26″

There are 17 different species, or kinds, of penguins.
Rockhopper
HEIGHT
21″–25″
Yellow-Eyed
HEIGHT
23″–30″
These penguins are the loudest. They sound like donkeys.
Magellanic
HEIGHT
24″–28″
African
HEIGHT
24″–28″
27

Macaroni
HEIGHT
21″–26″
Royal
HEIGHT
24″–28″
These penguins are the fastest swimmers.
Chinstrap
HEIGHT
27″
Gentoo
HEIGHT
27″–30″

Adelie
HEIGHT
22″–26″
Humboldt
HEIGHT
22″–26″
These penguins don't make a nest.
They carry their eggs wherever they go.
King
HEIGHT
37″
LARGEST
Emperor
HEIGHT
44″

Penguin Play

HOPPING: Rockhoppers can hop five feet high!

ROCKHOPPER PENGUIN

Q What do you call a penguin who surfs?

A A hang-ten-guin.

Life isn't always easy for penguins. But at least they look like they're having fun.

SINGING: Adults sing to their mates, and chicks sing for their parents.

MACARONI PENGUIN

SLEDDING: Penguins speed down icy hills on their feet and bellies to get somewhere fast.

KING PENGUIN

SURFING: Penguins surf through the waves. Sometimes they surf right from the water up onto land.

CHINSTRAP PENGUIN

BARB
Something sharp and pointy like a hook.

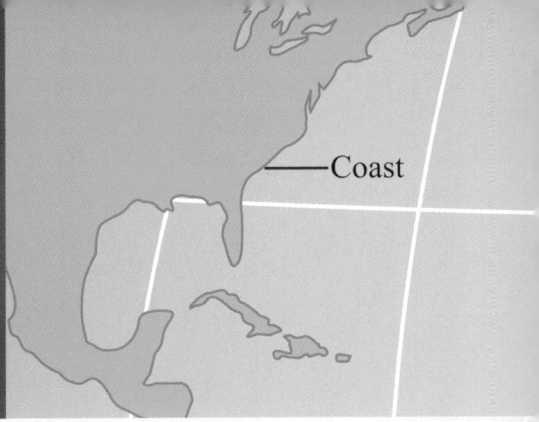

COAST
Where land meets water.

COLONY
A group of animals who live together.

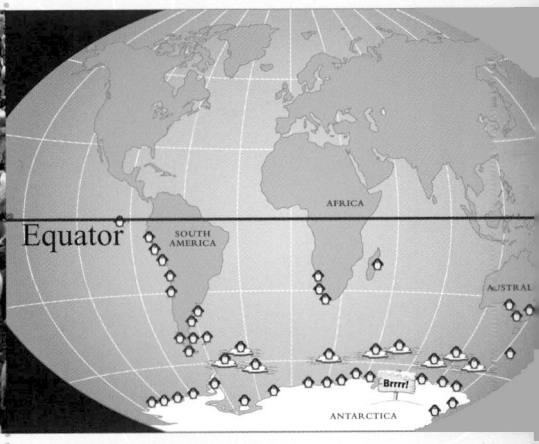

EQUATOR
An imaginary line halfway between the North and South Poles.

MARINE MAMMALS
Have fur and give birth to live young; unlike other mammals, they spend most of their time in the ocean.

WEBBED
Connected by skin.

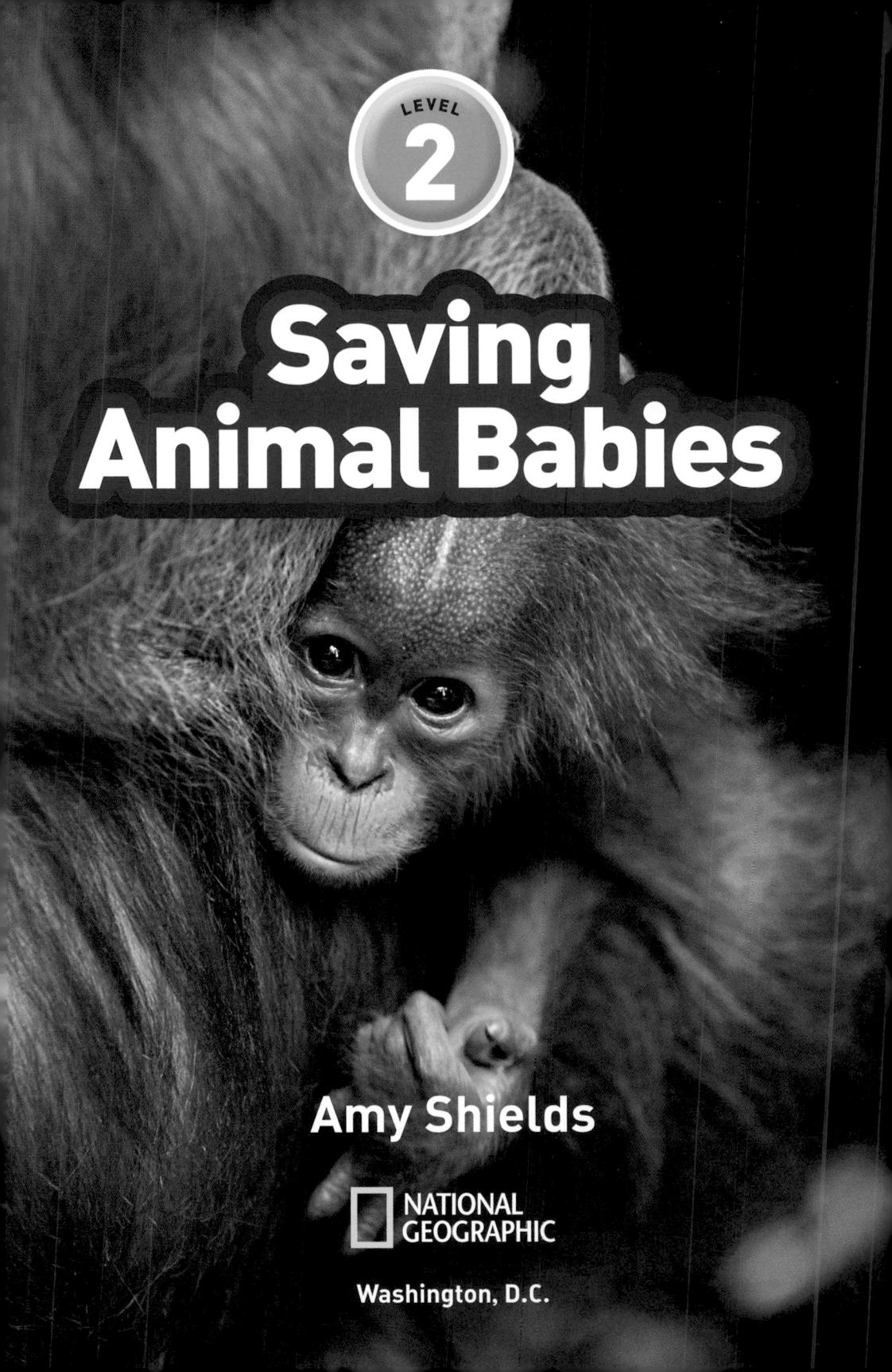
LEVEL
2
Saving
Animal Babies
Amy Shields
NATIONAL
GEOGRAPHIC
Washington, D.C.

Thanks to all the people who love and care for animals, especially Mary Fleming, Dr. Greg Mertz, Dr. Lori Perkins, Justine Brewer, and Dr. Laurie Gage. —A. S.

The publisher and author gratefully acknowledge the expert assistance of Ron Tilson of the Minnesota Zoo Foundation.

Published by National Geographic Partners, LLC, Washington, DC 20036.

Copyright © 2013 National Geographic Society

All rights reserved. Reproduction of the whole or any part of the contents without written permission from the publisher is prohibited.

NATIONAL GEOGRAPHIC and Yellow Border Design are trademarks of the National Geographic Society, used under license.

Design by YAY! Design

Paperback ISBN: 978-1-4263-1040-9
Library ISBN: 978-1-4263-1041-6

Photo Credits
Cover, Ron Kimball/Kimball Stock 1, Fuse/Getty Images; 2, Peleg Elkalay/Shutterstock; 4-5, Erik Beiersmann/dpa/Picture Alliance; 7 (UP), Horst Ossinger/AFP/Getty Image; 7 (LO), Chen Yingcai/Imaginechina; 8, Smithsonian's National Zoo; 9, Smithsonian's National Zoo; 11, Andrew Cunningham, Cummings School of Veterinary Medicine, Tufts University; 12, Andrew Cunningham, Cummings School of Veterinary Medicine, Tufts University; 13, Southwick's Zoo and Belinda Mazur; 15, Courtesy of Zoo Atlanta; 16, Courtesy of Zoo Atlanta; 17, Courtesy of Zoo Atlanta; 18 (UP LE), Vanderlei Almeida/AFP/Getty Images; 18 (UP RT), Suzi Eszterhas/Minden Pictures; 18 (LO), Martina Stevens, Houston Zoo; 19 (UP), John Macdougall/AFP/Getty Images; 19 (CTR), x99/ZUMA Press; 19 (LO), Steven Good/Shutterstock; 20, Alex Mustard/2020VISION/ Nature Picture Library; 22, © National Aquarium; 23, © National Aquarium; 24, Dr. Greg Mertz; 25 (UP), Dr. Greg Mertz; 25 (LO), Dr. Greg Mertz; 26, Dr. Greg Mertz; 27 (UP), Dr. Greg Mertz; 27 (LO RT), Dr. Greg Mertz; 27 (LO LE), Dr. Greg Mertz; 28 (UP LE), photomaster/Shutterstock; 28 (UP RT), Sarah2/Shutterstock; 28 (LO), v.s.anandhakrishna/Shutterstock; 29 (UP LE), Vitali Burlakou/Shutterstock; 29 (UP RT), Dimj/Shutterstock; 29 (CTR LE), Diane Macdonald/Getty Images; 29 (CTR RT), Picsfive/Shutterstock; 29 (LO), Marina Jay/Shutterstock; 30 (UP), Chen Shichuan/Imaginechina; 30 (LO LE), Ferry INDRAWANG/Shutterstock; 30 (LO RT), Simon Greig/Shutterstock; 31 (UP LE), Derek R. Audette/Shutterstock; 31 (UP RT), Dougal Waters/Getty Images; 31 (LO LE), Ekkachai/Shutterstock; 31 (LO RT), Mint Images RM/Getty Images; 32 (UP LE), Franco Tempesta; 32 (UP RT), Courtesy of Zoo Atlanta; 32 (CTR LE), Zurijeta/Shutterstock; 32 (CTR RT), Erik Beiersmann/dpa Picture-Alliance; 32 (LO LE), Andrew Cunningham, Cummings School of Veterinary Medicine, Tufts University;32 (LO RT), © National Aquarium; header used throughout, Potapov Alexander/Shutterstock; seal vocabulary, Vule/Shutterstock; tiger vocabulary, nemlaza/Shutterstock

Table of Contents

The Cubs Are Coming! 4

Eat, Sleep, Repeat! 6

A Long, Tall Baby 10

Wanted: One Hairy Mom 14

Toys for Tots 18

Saving a Seal Pup 20

Backyard Babies 24

Dos and Don'ts 28

Stump Your Parents 30

Glossary 32

The Cubs Are Coming!

It is a dark and quiet night at the zoo. The tiger is restless. The zookeeper thinks the tiger will have her babies soon. And she does.

Tiger babies are called cubs.

There are four new tigers in the world! Tigers are in danger of becoming extinct. That means every tiger is special.

Wild Word

EXTINCT: A group of animals that is no longer living

Eat, Sleep, Repeat!

This is the tiger's first litter of cubs. Some tigers don't take care of their first litter. Without help, the cubs could die. But caretakers at the zoo know what to do.

At first, the cubs only need to eat and sleep. Every three hours, the cubs drink warm milk.

The cubs have a blanket that smells like their mother. Sleep well, little tigers.

Wild Word

LITTER: All the babies born to an animal at one time

Q Which side of a tiger has the most stripes?

A The outside!

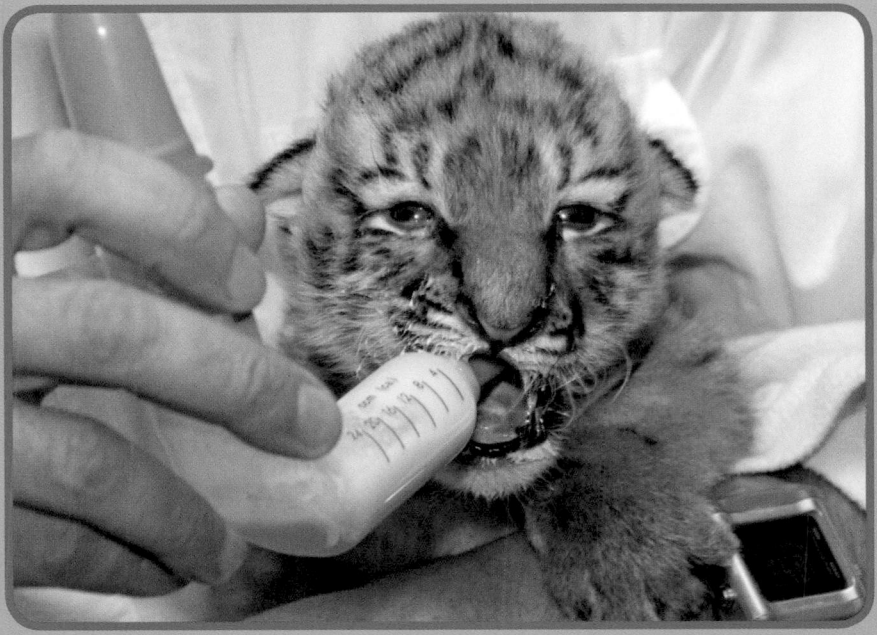

Would you like to try a chunky meat milk shake? The cubs are crazy for them.

First the veterinarian checks the cubs' baby teeth. They need to be strong and sharp to chew the chunks. Then the zoo chef buys jars of turkey baby food. He mixes it with milk and vitamins to make the milk shake.

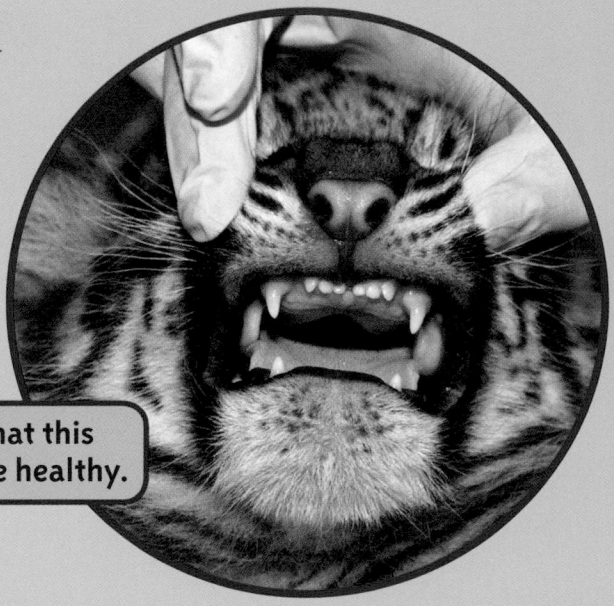

The vet sees that this cub's teeth are healthy.

A tiger cub is weighed to make sure it's growing well.

Now the cubs will grow even faster. One day they will be full-grown tigers.

Wild Word

VETERINARIAN: A doctor for animals, called vet for short

A Long, Tall Baby

Molly is three days old. She is an 80-pound, 5-foot-tall baby giraffe. This baby should drink three gallons of milk a day. But her mother cannot make milk for her.

Molly also has an infection. She needs help. She has to go to the hospital.

Wild Word

INFECTION: A sickness caused by a virus or bacteria

The vet feeds Molly milk. The tube in Molly's neck is held in place by a bandage.

Q Why wasn't the giraffe invited to the party?

A Because he was a pain in the neck!

The vet puts goat's milk in a giant baby bottle. She has to hold the bottle up high for Molly.

The vet puts a little tube in Molly's neck. It doesn't hurt and is an easy way to give Molly the medicine she needs.

Soon Molly is better and back with her mom.

Molly is healthy and growing. She is almost as tall as her mother!

Wanted: One Hairy Mom

Remy's mother got sick before he was born. She could not take care of Remy.

Orangutans need to be raised by other orangutans. Remy needed a foster mother to take care of him.

Madu is a grown-up orangutan. She never had a baby of her own.

But she had cared for two other orangutan babies that didn't have moms. Would Madu be a foster mother to Remy, too?

Remy is an orangutan baby. Young orangutans stay with their moms for five to seven years.

Remy snuggles with Madu.

With his blanket and toys, Remy went to meet Madu. It was love at first sight. Soon Remy climbed on Madu's back.

Remy watched Madu. Madu taught Remy what to eat. She showed him how to hang and climb. Remy learned how to be an orangutan.

Madu teaches Remy how to hang with one arm.

Q How do you catch an ape?

A Climb a tree and act like a banana!

Toys for Tots

All babies love toys. Zookeepers try to get the right toy for each baby.

Sloth babies cling to their moms. A stuffed pillow works, too.

Even the youngest monkeys can learn to hang from ropes or chains.

Elephants love splashing and swimming in water. A kiddie pool is lots of fun!

Polar bear cubs like to chase and pounce on a ball.

A treat frozen in ice is a puzzle for curious panda cubs.

Young tigers like to play with each other. Another tiger is better than any toy.

Saving a Seal Pup

Guinness is a gray seal, just like this one.

Q What did the ocean say to the seal?

A Nothing, it just waved!

Even ocean babies need help sometimes.

Wildlife rescuers saw a seal pup on the beach. Seals leave the water to rest. But this little guy was too thin. He didn't go back in the water. He was in trouble.

Rescuers wrapped him in a wet towel and took him to the hospital. They named him Guinness.

Wild Word

WILDLIFE RESCUER: Someone who saves wild animals from danger

Guinness had a broken jaw. The vets operated and put a wire in his jaw. The wire held the jaw together while the bone healed.

Three months later, Guinness could eat by himself again!

Guinness enjoys a frozen fish in ice—called a fishsicle.

It was time to go back to the water. Everyone cheered when Guinness scooted back to the ocean where he belonged.

Backyard Babies

Do you want to be a vet when you grow up?

You might want to be like Dr. Greg Mertz. People know him as the Odd Pet Vet. He takes care of all kinds of animals that need help.

Dr. Mertz helps a snake.

Q How do turtles talk to each other?

A By shell phone!

This three-month-old goose has a broken wing. The bandage works like a cast on a broken arm.

This painted turtle has a cracked shell. The bandage keeps away infection.

People bring hurt animals to Dr. Mertz. Many wild animals get hurt on roads. Luckily, Dr. Mertz can help most of the animals he sees.

Springtime is busy for Dr. Mertz. That's when many babies are born. Animal babies like to explore. Sometimes they get into trouble and need help.

Dr. Mertz to the rescue!

These opossum babies were found in the wall of a house.

An x-ray shows this bird swallowed a fishhook. Dr. Mertz took it out and saved the bird.

Raccoon cubs can live on their own after three months. Until then, Dr. Mertz keeps this one safe.

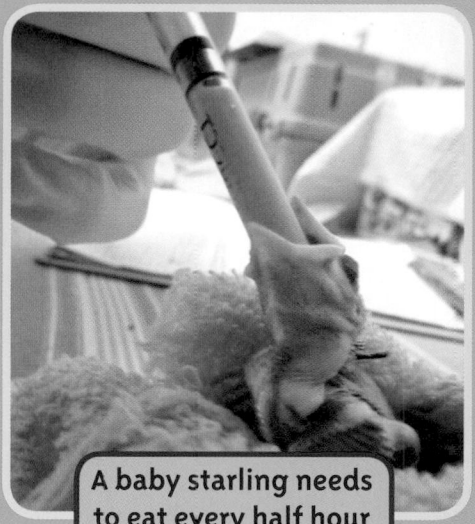

A baby starling needs to eat every half hour around the clock!

Dos and Don'ts

What can you do to help baby animals? Here are some dos and don'ts . . .

DO

slide a ramp in a pool if you see baby frogs in it. Then they can climb out safely.

DON'T

feed ducks and other birds bread. It's bad for them.

DO

wait 24 hours before rescuing a baby deer or bunny. The mother is probably nearby.

DO

tell an adult to call animal rescue if you see anyone hurting an animal.

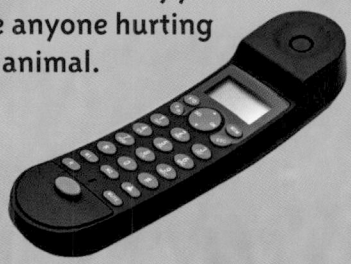

DON'T

adopt a wild animal. They do not make good pets.

DO

prevent pets from harming wildlife. Put a bell on your cat's collar. Keep your dog on a leash.

DO

pick up trash you see in the woods. Plastic bags and bottles can hurt animals.

DON'T

pick up a baby bird that is on the ground. Ask an adult or call a vet or the local Audubon Society for advice.

Stump Your Parents

Can your parents answer these questions about baby animals? You might know more than they do!

Answers are at the bottom of page 31.

1

When tigers are born, they _____.

A. Drink milk
B. Are hungry for meat
C. Don't sleep
D. Sing

2

What do young orangutans learn from older orangutans?

A. How to find food
B. How to hang and climb
C. How to be an orangutan
D. All of the above

3

What should you do if you find a baby bird on the ground?

A. Run away
B. Leave it alone and tell an adult
C. Bring it home
D. Give it some candy